GREEN AND GRAY

NEW CALIFORNIA POETRY

<table>
<tr><td>EDITED BY</td><td>Robert Hass
Calvin Bedient
Brenda Hillman
Forrest Gander</td></tr>
</table>

GREEN AND GRAY GEOFFREY G. O'BRIEN

UNIVERSITY OF CALIFORNIA PRESS
BERKELEY LOS ANGELES LONDON

University of California Press, one of the most distinguished
university presses in the United States, enriches lives around
the world by advancing scholarship in the humanities, social
sciences, and natural sciences. Its activities are supported by
the UC Press Foundation and by philanthropic contributions
from individuals and institutions. For more information, visit
www.ucpress.edu.

University of California Press
Berkeley and Los Angeles, California

University of California Press, Ltd.
London, England

Illustration on page iii: Ivy Grissom, *Rife Section I* (2005).
Reproduced by permission.

Library of Congress Cataloging-in-Publication Data

O'Brien, Geoffrey G. (Geoffrey Gordon), 1969 –
    Green and gray / Geoffrey G. O'Brien.
        p.   cm. — (New California poetry ; 20)
    ISBN 978-0-520-25018-5 (cloth : alk. paper)
    ISBN 978-0-520-25019-2 (pbk. : alk. paper)
    I. Title. II. Series.

PS3615.B75G74   2007
811'.6 — dc22   2006010238

Manufactured in Canada

16   15   14   13   12   11   10   09   08   07
10   9   8   7   6   5   4   3   2   1

The paper used in this publication meets the minimum re-
quirements of ANSI/NISO Z39.48 – 1992 (R 1997) (*Permanence
of Paper*).

FOR JOANNA

CONTENTS

ACKNOWLEDGMENTS

Some of the poems in this volume, sometimes in earlier forms, ap-
peared in the following publications: *1913: A Journal of Forms:* "Hysteron
Proteron"; *The Berkeley Poetry Review:* "Mixed Mode"; *The Boston Review:*
"On the Phantom Estate," "The Nature of Encounters," "To Classes";
Colorado Review: "At the Changing Villa"; *Conduit:* "A Difficult Summa-
ry," "Ajar," "Beginnings of Rounds," "To Be out of Sweden and"; *Crowd:*
"A Word with a Poem around It," "False Neutral"; *The Modern Review:* "A
Calendar," "Alieniloquy," "Amorous Poem," "Fountain," "In Re Others,"
"Objects in Portraits," "Realia," "The Bulletin of Lyon," "The New," "Ur,"
"Wall of Men and Women"; *No: A Journal of the Arts:* "Logic of Confes-
sion," "Man of Joy," "Sent Past Exhibits"; *Pequod:* "Several Endless State-
ments"; *River City Review:* "Paraphrase of Aragon"; *Volt:* "Deer Isle,"
"Some Versions of"; and *War and Peace 2* (O Books): "They Met Only in
the Evenings."

Thanks to my editors, Cal Bedient, Forrest Gander, and Brenda
Hillman; to all my students and colleagues; and to Jeff Clark, Timothy
Donnelly, Judith Goldman, Ben Lerner, and Stephen Smith.

Notes: "They Met Only in the Evenings" was composed using only
language from the USA PATRIOT Act; subsequently, one word per
line was replaced with a word from a translation of Jean Genet's
Querelle.

The last line of "In Re Others" condenses the last sentence of Aris-
totle's *Poetics.*

GREEN AND GRAY

SOME VERSIONS OF

There is no reason a poem would begin
with reference to the territory
with refrains to be used by all sides

No reason a poem would begin if
and only if or with refrains
for a territory already conquered

Invincible a shining example
of immediate environs of damage and
its image there is no reason a poem

Would begin the woods are white and black
green leaves blue at certain hours or
the woods differed a poem beginning

You the thing at either end of a gun
sundown or colony would begin as aftermaths
of persons no reason in or by a flow

Of pronouns of pronouncements of capture
a poem would begin as a play
of there is and drift away no reason

A poem would begin we brought all lights
home with us were porters at borders
in a day done slowly away with

No reason a poem would start
by censoring my shame or yours
at having a country or of the others

Would begin as expressive acts stills of time
headed in all directions in wartime or peacetime
solitary avoidable while snow fell

Would begin I am is asleep in the afternoon
returns to apartments waits in a change
steadily flashing would begin by describing

Continuous endless materials states of sky
neither mine nor someone else's epic fragments
neither beginning nor not no reason a poem would

Begin so much and so more or she hummed to himself
of the many forces these and other nights
of the things selflessly explained

As snow or fire no unreal season
a poem would begin by stating
by steadily flashing as utopia

Transmits its coordinates utopiates
headed in all directions no reason
the mean of a life and a moment is

The standard working day the mean of a life
and falling asleep the whole of summer
no reason a poem would begin

A whole day before winter whole summers before night
would be gone by night or touched lightly
in the dark would be abandoned there

Would be gone by not having come
would come to be used by all sides
would begin with reference to refrains

PARAPHRASE OF ARAGON

I hear I hear the world is there
It passes from people on the road
More than my heart I listen to them
The world is badly made my tired heart

Through courage or audacity
All goes its train nothing turns
One arranges oneself with the danger
The age comes without anything occurring

In a spring still dreamed as spring
One takes the hand which one crosses
Nods and puts the words on slate
Count who can the wasted time

All these faces these faces
I saw the unhappy ones so much
And what I've made is made for them
If not to waste my courage

If not to sing then to hum with the sun
So that the shade is made human
Like one Sunday a week
And the hope with the truth

I saw some so much who went away
They asked only warmth
They were satisfied with so little
They had so little anger

I hear their steps I hear their voices
Who say banal things
As one reads sometimes in the newspaper
Like one says on an evening at home

What one makes of you men women
Tends to sharpen and is early worn
And your broken appearances
To look to the heart of you tears me away

The things go as they go
From time to time the ground trembles
Misfortune resembles misfortune
It is deep deep deep

You would like with the blue sky to believe
I know it this feeling
I believe in it also sometimes
Like the lark with the mirror

I believe in it sometimes I acknowledge it to you
While not believing my ears
I am truly your similar
I am quite similar to you

With you like the beach parts
Like poetry in blood
Like the always wounded fingers
I am truly your similar

I would so much have liked to help you
You who seem another myself
Words that I sow on a black wind
Who knows if you hear them

All is lost and nothing touches you
Neither my words nor my hands
And you go your path
Without knowing what my mouth says

Your hell is however mine
We live under the same rule
And when you bleed I bleed
And I die in your same links

This time is what time makes it
I would have liked so much however
To gain you with losing myself
To have been perhaps useful

It's a modest and insane dream
It would have been better to conceal it
You'll be taken to me from above ground
Like a glint to the bottom of a hole

THREE SEASONS

Winter, it was the winter all
the usual things happened,
I have forgotten what
would travel from the north
as a series seen from above
or from below, and the followers,
the flowers, I tore them up
the next summer, or rather
before or immediately after
and thought no more about it.
But then the summer, plans
to sign a contract, the summer
came back for what it was:
a small sprinkling of rue
and a yellow fantasy
and we were invited. It appeared
tall and swaying and deaf
to appeals, and the winter following,
this was the arrangement—
first one and then into
another not yet there,
many years of this refrain
and all the productions within it
coming to mean more
of an intimacy between
musical instruments and still lifes
you lose yourself in again

and probably have now,
what objects have known
in their one dark winter afternoon.
Still visited there
by everything else together
they complete the effect, a distance
which the next day took form.
That winter stopped and probably
on account of summer a spring,
spring with a sturdy fringe
and a local reputation,
it's outside, in various rooms
and looks at everything,
a few lilacs in awkward
positions, but they were alright,
it was summer, very strong,
passing organizations,
that never finished anything
and ended in making
all this, cold coals
of wildflowers, wars
at the centers, they go on for years
burning near the front
and from below.

THE NEW

From that time onwards
                        one day it happened
during that time
                        for so long
after the departure,
                        a few days after
when I returned
                        whenever and wherever
now, returning to my subject,
                                    after that which I described,
after the battle of conflicting thoughts,
                                            after this strange transformation,
  when I had finished this,
                            when I had written this
as many people had guessed,
                                then it happened,
when this had circulated,
                            when I had discussed it,
not many days after that,
                            a few days after this,
after this delirious dream,
                            at this point someone
of whom I have spoken,
                        after this I began,
I was still composing this.
                            Now, according to the way of reckoning time,

after I had departed,

    from now on,

when this had been composed,

     when I had written this,

when the day came,

    afterwards, for some time,

from then on wherever

     the sight of this had an effect

the appearance of this wrought in me,

      in opposition to this,

after this tribulation,

    later, after this

and to this end.

THE BULLETIN OF LYON

Waiting in a café for a candidate
on a day made up from a larger script,
the way the lion awaits the rose
across an intervening age,
the way the earth waits to be used
with the inward certainty of bells or execution,
in the renewable source of that certainty,
across its flowers and feral areas,
peals and sentences, every friday
at noon waiting in the café
for the candidate, who never comes,
who clearly has seen and yet never comes.
In a chair at the table in a corner of the square,
the gray of the stone and green of the trees,
among a people hypnotized by sounds
as they could be by each other
were there acknowledgment or persons
were visible, imaginary animals
carrying sentences around their necks
towards those in the glare of the road.
Sitting reading at a table every friday
at noon, the date on the paper, the real
hypothetical orchards
from which the paper comes, the rustling
of the date. How long with the bells
and the changing clientele
to be waiting correctly, the spoon and cup,

sun through a glass in the air, sparrows flying
from here to somewhere else, for how long
with coffee or wine, the flatness of the square,
of a mute white tablecloth.
Sitting recovering its weave alone
for an instant only the past of it
coming together then the labor gone
in a glow of white almost blue
taking wing against trees, crowds, commerce,
again a set of lines
poor as the system to date.
And on its streets how often
to be moved and moving through its people
who surely have heard and yet continue
to form up in overlapping rings,
who are the antidote and symptoms,
wares and news, who've been told
to be themselves and yet look innocent.

At a table in a chair facing out on the square,
gray of the stone and green of the sounds at noon,
sitting in young sounds of errands,
in the imperial flower of a partial answer
lying between all people,
between all and each, and the rest of it
so much distributed sun in the trees
planted at points along the square.

How long to sit and how long be faithful
to the shapes taken by the future, live
in the renewable source of that certainty—
lemons in water, waiter's sleeve, slates
the birds rise from to be together
above the square, flights in formation,
simple hypnotic returns.
And how often against the surround to be waiting,
ignored, in the old sounds of industry,
sounds though desired that are not the reply,
sitting, eating, served by the one if neglected
inside vague errands of the others,
hypothetical, imaginary,
tracing the tablecloth into the trees.
The idea, long in coming, is itself
simple as a flower opening,
too simple to be heard but still
opening, the flower a crowd carries
behind its ear, continuing to grow
in a year the year leaves behind.
An idea of waiting for things to be lent
and made useful, ordained in the ground
no matter how exotic and whether
orange-red or red-orange,
bell-shaped, hanging from a crown
of upright pointed leaves at the top
of the stem one becomes

in the absence of the candidate
who, at noon every friday, an unfilled glass,
hasn't yet come to the café,
come yet for reasons thought loses
in the glare of every other day.

A DIFFICULT SUMMARY

First premonitions of invisible lights
and then the potential to serve as reference.
First all colliding accidents joined in the senses
then all possible commonplace books.
First the false parts of real people
affirmed as presences at night.
First music, which can only assemble them
in where they hear it to be, then the desire at night,
above an empty store, not to live
in only one room of the house. First
the impropriety of thought then its fall
in shared veils, groups of pairs
peripheral vision turns to souvenirs.

First apertures in a face-encrusted crowd
music can only assemble like a thought,
from no previous record into it, from
the commonplace parts of real colliding people,
then false books affirmed in the senses at night,
a premonition of invisible lights
housed in the desire for reference. First confusion
of silence with inwardness, then of thought with ourselves.
First the accident of thought then its music
and then its potential to serve the stores and crowds.
First play and display then broken record of faces,
of many are the few, many are the few . . .
First not to live in empty reference, no and then

IN RE OTHERS

There is this to say: so much
for living a life alone among others,
in the throes of others as they come into view;
they suggest human states but are this damage—
difficult months, an old yard
near the turn events take. There is this
to say: you walk out with into them again

mitered with the same reds and anguished gains,
you the subject of an art of others
variously disguised and as loyally opposed.
You the thing moved from sun into shade, sun
into sun, speeched along other shining paths
to a barrier the words come from. You can say anything now:
the word *A*, the word *vessel*, the word *with*, the word *cracks*, the words *in it*,

they're remembered, and then they enter where they were:
a shrinking commons otherwise known as
onsets of the past; they're remembered and then spring
aimlessness of green that reappears as comments
on the solution of an eye, recognitions
you can say everything now: that whole stands for part
for as long as they constitute a single language.

Interlude: if only we no longer lived
in the old systems of the future and
it were evened out among them

and they kept it that way
and you were one of them, there were
no prepositions, lips were eyes
and, early summer, we could hear each other speak.

And a portion of the talk is with others, serpentine
at certain times, the writing of hearing it said,
walking around discursively and of course
waving goodbye, reversing a blow, an instant
that proves, like the others on either side,
no motion but will fit the air,
not a vector of a sentence it doesn't hold

without enclosing. Asked and answered, the thing moved
through the end of the day, when it darkens,
when the cashier is in delirium,
a violent nothing at the pulse points of the house,
nodding to the others slowing at the table,
fire-trance without need of fire,
a discontent without content

falling toward the dark of the other pronouns
through rites of sleep familiar and not,
a little lamp when its oil runs dry
no longer responsible till morning.
You wake up in their world: summer

full of brown poles, real as elsewhere,
in which there is this to say: so much

for days that return to make stupidity
seem recent, for transcripts of birdsong lifting the sun
above a pleasure in self-interest, a sun that lights
others coming to the fore, other others
back and forth across a shadow line,
across all costs all arrangements, so many so much
the feeling is of old bells about to ring

with the vigor of their era. The latest others
set out among life living in states
but being the days, the seven sails of the factory,
attitudes both dismissive and afraid
instantly refiltering stranger and friend,
each message to be entered and sent. And most of these
things when they need to be said can be said with a ship

and a wave, with only and also, in tabular form
ecstatic as a train schedule. The feeling is
of the other side of the beginning of a bridge,
imaginary numbers, scratches on a table.
You recite conflicting commands, near
words of a song; still hours
before having to meet them and wonder whether

there will be even this left over
to say: so much but too little, enough,
the others sent out among likes living instead
for the dates of their open appointment. Synonyms
which, when they need to be said, can be said with a train
and some tracks, with in lieu and less so, in fabular terms
happy as a bill of lading. And of that you

who speaks in your sleep of the states to come,
who arranges the reign of others for as long as they do
simply by continuing, of that center
shifting through the rest of them . . . there is this to say:
staring into the sun and shade of others
is the mystery of traditions and of towns,
the one chronic fight between magistrate and priest;

also a bee in a well, the edges of islands,
any meeting place of the one life and the other
and the rekillable flowers that grow there
as though to say: there is this. There are these
true differences growing from and towards
a single past, a winter in which all are the others.
So much for problems and their solution.

LOGIC OF CONFESSION

All photos are taken out of remorse
Are of where the senses go when closed
All photos are still lifes of the senses
Are at least of lost faith in the senses
I've therefore seen all possible photos
They aren't like my experience
I see them as being all the same
All photos are the remorse of the senses
Subtracted from experience
I therefore see them as similar
And I prefer some to the others
Some still lifes to the other still lifes
I like those that are of perfect fruit
The blood on the ground, the yes
I love these fruit piled up in the photos
They aren't as rough as my senses
Where grapes happen but oranges occur
Inequity and difference unavoidable
In the photos they all pile together
The fruit and the tanks and the smile
They pile together for the master they serve
The plum and the star and the wave
All photos serve as a yes to a master
A yes unable to be said
The master unseen in the photo

I still prefer not to see this master
Therefore I love photos, or "photographs"
Especially those in which there are fruit
The fruit that have been taken out
of the life of which I'm a mistress

REALIA

My people, provided I have one, are like women and men.
Their dreams are like dreams filled with things:
citizens, coins, their faces, flames and signs,
snow, air, earth, sighs, sun.
All morning each emphasis of field
reveals its portion of the unpredicted,
the heart of the surface flares. Fragrance
is emitted wherever flowers are.
They're divided in the hedge of afternoon
where also gates open, streets ripen
with figures; one comes before, one after,
passing like expressions on a face.
Most orders resemble this: you watch
a friend remember someone else's
unapproachable beauty then both recede
in countless local ways time passes.
There are golden claims about this face,
all simplicity and all subtlety;
in countless local ways it's not to be
looked at directly, is sunlight falling up streets,
letters fading for want of explanation,
a collection of objects useful for teaching.
They lie there like different faces
in a dream about days, each one
there with the force of sun in an alley:
one face that says there's nothing
between languages, another

that claims the difference lies
in being led versus coming after,
and a third that argues
within this time all others are
now to be dealt with as exceptions.
One cannot imagine now except as all parts,
as inventory, case, self-explanation.
It was to be entire days and is
the time of writing, impossible enterprise
whose crimson cloth has been removed.
In this way a friend a provocation and
the sun only a portion of all it reveals.
Wooden boards, windows, clothing, screen.
You walk by a river in the anarchy
of mid-translation and are continuous,
remembering the claims of friends, the one
who comes first and the one who comes after, emphases
written in the surface. One can imagine now
how social the spring is, how residential and endless.
Beatrice is here, emitted wherever flowers flare.
All afternoon while a perfume rises
out of private gardens through the promise
of a future intrinsic to its return.
The flowers and the streets, two views
of the same material, two things one can
walk by a river thinking helplessly of.
This is the prediction of Beatrice: all things

are simple and subtle, material and unpredicted,
helpless, divided, idyllic, claims and flares,
soldiers, children, anarchy, time unapproachable.
This is the other prediction of Beatrice:
each night evening emerges.
Exactly this exuberance
brought us together with those we used to know.

UR

I saw the only man there is
walking home across a stage
Pushed to do so
Coming home from someplace else
as though inheriting
lights coming on over doors
Looking with the sense of having been
put there on purpose to survive
to be equal to a turning point
where something else was
where it was thick and now
the sense of no one following
Future perfect purple-brown
of twilight both ahead and behind
I saw the obvious houses
neither following nor stopping dead
the yield of a place in departure
curves of trees across the stage
The nature we were taught of
shadow of a magnet on the grass
some think will soon disappear
the grass in the middle of its flight
from thought to neglect
returning again when needed
Doubtless to return again
I walked home across a stage
like weather beginning to

and here where myself in the distance
where apparitions and obligations
and a sense of being extended as
and in the depths of exchanges like changes
stories of the marketplace
audible worlds and their urns
I see a woman who'll soon disappear
after having her part
in a rhythm like grasses

MAN OF JOY

Unless I am much mistaken everything
is music, but that's not really right.
What can one say of a desire
for new connections other than that it swells
up out of feeling happy, wanting
to play, not knowing how to,
traveling with a companion in the dark.
I didn't consciously remember this
main scene but I find it everywhere,
the portrait of a porter who no longer
acts as such, he takes off his uniform
at the border and becomes another passenger.
What other traveling companions
through sound and through dark can be hoped for?
I can say only this of the way sights
won't lend themselves to lasting judgments—
I'm not appealing to any verdict
from a martyred instrument or painting
of last things or the dark of last summer
falling within a normal range
of expression. I wouldn't like to say
what I do think but I'll be happy to tell you
in a foreign language that it involves
old men and silhouettes, the opinions of women
on trains, moving through a barren area.

To be happy I think of as
new editions of the same world
swelling or rising from a fur-lined machine.
I think of a marriage with distress,
silence as not speaking and writing
as silence in bed, also blurred words
at the end of the month, certain turns of the head
made to no one, paint still running,
gestures unaware of their power
to persuade. I think of fortifications
against hills. This is the usual way
and I think of forgetting and hurrying
off to the library to look up the links
between green skies, green roses, and the bliss
that comes off a sea, I hear the nothing
I have to say until I begin.
All children can understand this,
especially the unattended child
exhaling in the closet of bed
who's already been listening
with a sense that talking isn't to scale
if done by someone else—a train
has passed by, not to be painted.
It would be no distortion to say
nothing happens unless that child is present
to see or hear it. This is happiness:

a place no longer anything else
as the drying picture chases it away.

I think of the village which liberates itself
into the silent spruces, of
continuations on the train
whose windows are portraits; I am not
at a loss for examples. A place will often
come up to me as triangles and bars
and the following idea will be suggested:
it's a parable of isolation to remember
the name of a painting while traveling
and a parable of sound to say it
under whistlings or dull roars the train makes
while pulling meaning and music out
of the last station. I think of youth and age
coming up to me, not knowing how
to play and then knowing how not to.
I look at a watch or in a bag and often
I see a lion vividly before me.
This is the child gypsies have stolen
from his crib whom I'd like to give
another life, the mouth, tongue, and teeth
of a useless head. I immediately
associate head with a woman one carries
out of a burning train, who was once a girl

and now works for a family whose name
I forget, it has to do with gold.

And what of not leaving the apartment very much,
of writing or reading an entire book
without leaving the house? This is happiness:
to forget an appointment, utter a little cry
and a moment later, in the breakdown,
remember it doesn't exist, the girls are hiding
in the spruces. If this is a little like death
or staying home from work so be it,
I've carried a laughing dog in my arms
out of a fire and into the "trees"
and now can remember exactly whatever
associations there are and whatever
rhythms they possess, and if they in turn
make me think of rocks mostly moss,
labor, death, and sleep, a bird of prey
the color of a ticket on a train,
girls at the door and a boy in a yard,
still all the strands change lengths when you move,
I can't say why this is, and when you don't
it can all be thwarted in bed.

FOUNTAIN

There is no such thing as the abrupt
Doubleness is the first plural
The abrupt comes in many forms
of which doubleness is one overture
The world occurs as time enforces it
In return it recognizes time
Again the bottom predicts a top
Fresh sources resemble each other
Goods are exchanged throughout the day

REVALUATION OF PURPLE

A mixture of the two ways blood
and sky intrude and what they do
when there—they grow old, and consecrated.
There are more recent works than purple
but they're dyed swearing, done
for a particular effect,
they don't fuse two gardens
in a single role or become forensic
as purple does at its best. All
emotions halt before it, words
return to their sources, time is singed.
I'm thinking of a sail for a boat
or the liveliest part of defective painting,
something that might have kept going.
Not because it's cut from a radiant hollow
but because it's frank
in disallowing other movement
the color circulates, a clue to the senses
as they themselves are. I'm thinking of
the death of variation and
I have in mind something neither
tranquil nor violent if necessary
now, a beating place
that points out what's wrong about places.
They're a caricature of living
in a larger world, as purple itself does.
I didn't like purple but now I do,

it's a kind of barrier on the frontier
of incidents, still not clear
how it was moved there
to lend shine to a bleeding edge
and complicate disappointment
or why the debt feels new.

ON THE PHANTOM ESTATE

Money is the sun at night, spirit
is a parrot. What is the thing?
A public assembly on a hill,
a hill the color of sage or money.
The assembly sounds like birds
and what it says is that
in another world we will not matter.
At night the hill is the color of night,
sage is the color of night
and money sleeps in the thing.
It's even trained to say this thing
whose upper limit is another
and whose lower limit music,
the sound of the sun in that other world.
To get there a coin is placed in the mouth
of the dead—this the silent music
of the thing, the untrained speech of the dead.
They are deported into space as spirit
and reassemble under the hill.
The sun returns, and the birds.

OBJECTS IN PORTRAITS

In the uncertain light of the first person
anything made is embarrassing.
Sometimes one wants to leave the city
and some of those times one does
and at those times one is an afforested I—
the dampness as exhilarating
as why it is and the absence of houses
a gleefulness best not confused
with any of the birdsong and light on the earth
and it would be a mistake to call it
"the light of the earth"—only I would make this mistake.
There is gold here and there on a path,
suggesting the attempt to supplement
is the contribution, a laughable one.
Laughter, the light of the earth.
It's made, though not a thing, then expended
dreamily, a fabric without a back
falling on all the sounds of a place
perceived in walking through splintering woods—
the general noise of nature most resembles
laughter, while that of a city is
the scaffolding together of frames.
It isn't, but if it were one would be

awake, it would be beyond sense to say
small questions love the woods,
that even the most witless functions

are refreshed in entering precincts
where running time is bred with its parts
and understood to be imaginary.
Is bred to produce the equally passing sense
of being there. Which is suggested
in the legend of the senses
reascending to their proper dwelling place
as discontinuous sounds, and shadows
occurring in a small enough part
of the total setting they admit only
a first person, made so as to live there.
An embarrassment which is also the earth's:
here and there the same things
happen, a single iris on a path,
the path still mistaken for time.
During its session one finds
to find is to turn, to turn to look
for a place that isn't artificial
even if it is jagged, jagged as the laughter
one partly is laughing
for as long as houses are made of wood.

TO BE OUT OF SWEDEN AND

to know how Sweden is, to see leaves
change color without appropriate sound,
to go to work, a finger in the mouth of the day,
to think of how the leaves look on workdays
in Sweden when the sun allows them
to approach an unrevealed maximum, to look
like something other than motion or rest
still striven for, to relocate in place
to track the meaningless blaze of leaves changing color
in Sweden without appropriate sound, to think
all color the immediate memory of black,
to think of Sweden as unable to be tried
from its past, where the gate stood, the thought lived,
to live days without consequence
in which leaves retreat to further visibility
during the hours of work, days not just
for recruits or the calling in of students, days
that fall in anticipation of the past, today
and the others, released from standard duty,
to be underneath their sky, adjective
which describes the world, to be in the Sweden
of that world, in the sun-changed leaves of that Sweden
during the hours of work, to think, each time
a new thing is seen, each thing seen
is second of three, fragments of a great unconfession,
to put off confessing, to count the gold auras
around bushes on cliffs by the sea while others work,

to see the sun across these colored surfaces,
to say of leaves they represent everything
except themselves, the total obstinate trait,
to call work the opera of that trait,
to hear an absence of jets overhead
with obligations to other destinations
unable to be tried, to go to work again
shining a diffidence at the great group,
the I-they-we, to run from the dead
into evening, to know how Sweden is,
where spring must end but summer can't begin,
the unplanned days joining up
in long looks across heights.

ALIENILOQUY

Spots instead of points,
faint lines and flaws
where participations develop
and decisions get made, flowers
with studded pits too technical
to believe anything other than
charcoal gray with blotches of white,
fashioned without threats.
In the way a rich past forms,
serial, without apologies,
the definition of this month
drowned groin of winter under spring,
instruments handed over
for use in later tests.
Whether it's a lined shout
from the nonhuman agents
of gessamine or the radioactive
bid of woodbine, graceful and bashful,
my purpose as a mourner is
not to be such, glowing,
the soil a friendly wall
where almost familiar lies,
divides and widens, a vague attention
to the pain of a set of aims.
Time passes. In an alternate garden
nothing is yet done.
To alter the speed of clouds or companions

is no longer an ambition.
I'm interested now in something other
than outcomes, instead,
so beautiful I forgot to tell you,
sun on moss—to let it happen or
happen again, a noun
for sun where sun before,
going cold as it approaches;
about what a hall could contain
in the design on its carpet
of the half-lives of pleasure.
Then on through faint thoughts of others,
embroidery, scars, the last lines of a role.

And I feel guilty about rising up
the stem of a pose and then forgetful.
Wells, unexpectedly. Outrage at objects
a mild affection by nightfall;
the lamp flowers, once is twice.
I guess at what will come next
and know I'm guessing, my double role
to guess and be the one who guesses.
I feel the smile of my part as daylight
opens out to regard, inverts over coffee,
its depths an assumption moving makes
while thinking things repeated
are pleasing. And that all things unlit

are therefore yet to be used
in the space of encounter.
These things scripted because they happen,
wild radish, tournaments, lead,
but I'm interested, looking for a point
alone or apart, one whose surprise
is kept at the yet of connection.
That it would be customary there
to measure out the distances at which
speech sounds like wolves in a building.
Rumor or vibration, a partial match,
happening near but not in.
Or sleeping upstairs again
in the open hall that is
April, laughing a little
at distinctions in past accounts,
happy behind an olive curtain
to be making that mistake
for which honey is no redemption;
even its trapped time
giving way to colored lines
and the lines to rewards
from an unexpected source
I want to say is also
the stiff month magenta returns
where, instead of children,
propagations and flights

by which I extend a tenderness
towards efforts usually left to spring,
I who am to myself less pensive
than waiting in knowledge
of a friend who's sure to come.

AMOROUS POEM

The calla lilies have arrived, they come
the size of vague hymns if different
in shape, they weren't made or thought, they grew
without fidelity, hence the open
impassable cup and inability to speak,
to move out beyond an ordered length
as partially free persons. Instead a yellow
spike in a white sheaf on a green stalk,
things friends abandoned.

BEGINNINGS OF ROUNDS

From wherever it abides permanently
Towards a sudden dearness of near objects
In search of a mood beyond the range of houses
After the other stories have left the source
Again like a servant passing through rooms
Weather shows up over versions of towns
What was it to have the weather again?
It was having a face caught consistently
On currents of the neck, to grow bored with surprises
Something repeated at itself in nature
Each moment curfew and lamentation
Recanting the new life in clouds
It was thinking about ash and dying with friends around
To stand up again in a circular light
Of being custodian and journalist
To the fighting sense of going towards a spring
Not new but different from the old
Intermittence of little half-sung roads
After music has been in a room
It would be to know the trick of administrations
It would be to know the trick of administrations
From the point of view of those inside them

Who sing an international of decent feelings
That a face is a thing through which sound passes
Horrible and cozy, to have it and to leave it
Proud of having waited in such a fine point

A brow sometimes felt to be a ship's interior
A boat sometimes felt to be a cloud
The speaking of night over certain buildings
Who sing this international of how
It's tempting to be useful and tempting to lie down
Inside the active spin, in the penalty
For having thoughts, to wait there for
A sky and its sequels, the funeral speed
Of smoke seen to spread from a moving train
What would it be to have weather for the first time?
It would be as it is without having waited
It would be not really getting anywhere
And a changing sameness of the air
In which most people don't know each other
Though all are present, brought together in apartness
Thoughts of spring lead only to other thoughts
New ones not different from the old
It would not be embarrassing that morning came

DEER ISLE

Maybe rust and flowers are friends,
maybe axes drifting swiftly into wood
happens at times, perhaps things are
hard by other things, a car in the woods.
The country is large, jammed with dimension
and swift. I think the American people
know there are flowers speeding through
the woods and maybe waiting there. It's night
on an island belonging to this country,
rusted away from its mainland. Flowers
under the sign of life are looking for housing
and springing from the earth in the woods
that thrives on both consensus and dissent.
I think the American people know
how to collect and be one at a time
the crowd as it happens to drift, the island
under the sign of swiftness, a garden
in the back of the car. I think rust knows
night collects from unused alternatives.
The night over time becomes this night—
black leaves, descriptions without terms,
descriptions fully only. I think
the American people know this night
thrives on swiftly driving through the woods,
on flowering and ending, being one at a time.
It is the island and then the island is,
the island is friends with return, looking for housing,

trying dimension. It's once again
exposed by its trees to the dawn hard by,
part of a country that happens to thrive
on night and day, jammed with alternatives.
Under the sign of life night drifts away
into the mainland of time. The American
people becomes this people, this
large thing as easy as speaking of flowers.
One can say of their parts, I saw them and I see them
and one can be misquoted verbatim. It is
as it is, the driftwood and waves,
a wreck in the woods. I think the American
people understand these descriptions of gardens.

AT THE CHANGING VILLA

It would be nice to sleep here and think
of farms where everything gets done early,
men and women born without destination
into a stalwart reagency of flowers,
gathering them before they crowd the path
and the path leading in more than two directions,
beams driven free from an eye.
It would be an easy struggle to live
in a house built just by mentioning it,
the focused, involuntary rhythm
of a fire going on inside
part summer and part pain,
the flames not saying what they'll say next,
the contents of the room caused to run along
the walls as shadows—they're the children of your money
as you are, the far inks—hard to ignore
and harder still to consider. The this is
problem of senses confined to a head:
each runs back into the rest
without fear of being detained.
Like leaving a woman or a man,
watching the form of the flames one pays
less attention to their heat than to
clauses of an interfered-with air,
brief attempts at summoning
the summer morning where roads sprang away
to a permanent practice. It seemed certain a person,

the first, would be at the end of one, however
no way to tell if this is true.
Still, it's a privilege, a steady forgetting,
to stand here looking at the flowers
while thinking about the flames. That summer
when you look at things: one or the other
a set of instructions and one the thing they raise,
altering as the phrase is read aloud—
there are no "last houses"
after which the docile fields begin,
instead a series that comes from having been
many things, other things, others—

A WORD WITH A POEM AROUND IT

Rhythm opposes any instant of itself.
So too the tree that dumps itself
over a hedge lives in general time
beyond the concerns implied by sounds,
doesn't resemble any instant of itself,
can no longer be recognized as
a set of independences there run together
to form a forward-facing bust of age.
So too nights induced to be serene
curve around the features, preparing them
to be once more deliberately overheard.
Once again work has been done while you sleep.

SEVERAL ENDLESS STATEMENTS

Sunlight whose image is my thoughts
every day returns, and with it the speed
with which interest and uselessness return;
I keep forgetting my life is invocations
made without belief, set down
as such, a wind from the west, I forget
it continues this way: new, aligned with what's seen,
shut out, tired, in retreat, understanding
the little there is, exchanging it for sense;
reintroductions of the two
to each other as nearness
of another's blood during speech
in which all things are far; far as film,
healthcare, water, humor, fear
of being lived; sleep, the division into spring
and summer, remembering something
in the arms of something else; remembering nothing,
Detroit, Louisiana, a veteran, the rain,
what a few can order from afar;
errands, sex, reading, fruit, reprieves,
invocations made despite belief
in the relative comfort of a bed,
timed with day and night helplessly
in sync, the animal life, the life of pets;
a hysterical frankness with strangers, lies of tone
and lies of content, neither known to be so
while sent on their way, meetings with

commuters' eyes, dawn, voting, not,
transport to the pageant, fear of sleep;
friends, refusing to see what is seen,
aligned with the old, part of it, alone,
tired, on the phone, on a plane, trying
to keep the shape of the sheet in the air,
folding the limits of feelings into the feelings themselves,
sad after similar sadnesses;
dawn, a felon, a library, days
spent reading the poem of talking to strangers,
familiar attitudes, standing, looking down,
an unshared moving along; clouds, stress,
a face in the faces; new lines, lines,
the marks of having made them; chagrined
would be the word, remembering having
forgotten before, chagrined would be the word

After noticing a change in the meaning of the word
"ironic," she sat at home making the air
flow around her exactly as before.
It seemed people were becoming more comfortable
with an intention larger than any of them
and its consistent disappearance among them.
When something went wrong, say a woman
was born and grew up or boys limped
along the avenues with guns to their heart,
the clearness of the air would be doubled.
It was ironic, as it was that the church
remained white at the end of a little street,
glowing with waiting like the beach and the factory.
Coincidence that no one was seen
entering or leaving, that everyone was
already where they were going or where
they were meant to be, through days for getting up
as the condition of not being asleep,
nights spent behind a face—

                                        and the open sum
of days and nights gliding forward like a priest
between pews, a tradition that now goes on alone
without practitioners. Just so the world
crept on by, perfecting being watched.
This a thing best done in the anonymity
of silence, the state flower of speech
then its ultimate irony. She had noticed

that some people break the silence by saying "It's me,"
as night would fall across a doorway
with its many incitements and accusations,
their voice a sound of deference to their own voice,
a sleepy readiness not to be theirs
or any other, the cellar no one had noticed
was there, a little larger than its expectation.
Sleep does come to them, one thing
that can't be rehearsed; it resembles
again running out of things to say
in half the neglected cities,
one then two at a time,
and waiting there in hopes the world would act.

FALSE NEUTRAL

After this we'll never speak again,
will fool around in fountains, look up
at the sun, after that won't know the sun
by its difference from the trees, from the air,
will be knowing how not knowing that,
sleepy still upon waking, after conclusions,
will forget to be after them and then, a pain,
remember not to, be, no longer look
promptly in nature for a hidden statue,
not interested in finding it, not interested.
Will ignore the tunnel a face makes over time,
will ignore all limits except the last,
wake up into sun-through-the-trees
more golden than grass and greener than gold,
desiring that which is as if it were not.
Wake up in the downward fountain of the sun
for several days other than those to come—
strictly floating, repairing sudden circles—
will think of not speaking as a dry fountain
out past the last corrupted text,
in demands the same as being there, will think
to walk around confusing light and sound
with only the later set of faculties.
Won't do so, will sleep instead
after losses which are not the first
inside a promise of demise, its protractions,
will dream of reading by a fountain, clear syllables

that follow in the wake of sentences, syllables
misconstrued by the senses to be silent
for as long as the senses run silent.
Will come to finding discarded examples of these,
sound of the sun tunneling through time
lost in the feelings it brings through the trees
of a statement, interrupted.
And in the pain of a path through white
wake on both sides of the time before
feeling meant to know not yet,
cordially pouring forth from that place
towards a field where a play could be held,
from knowing how to knowing that
after this exactly like before
to live several threatened running totals,
watch the sun avoid its past,
turn and go into it, remind ourselves
to look away as though not interested.

A LITTLE OBJECT

To believe the thing desired not
a thing but a sudden range of gestures
practical as sunlight.
                    You saw it once
turning at a fair, a force, a breeze,
an art that doesn't need to be here.

SPRING STRUGGLE

Not a malice in the orchard
but a memory of that malice,
not in speaking directly of it
but in simply hearing speech.
I wrote a speech about that orchard,
must have written it to remember so well.
Near it was a mine though only
in my descriptions of it, a thought of
how kind the mouth of a mine can seem
next to an orchard. The mouth can seem
an ear also, for what I think
the orchard would say in my descriptions.
If it spoke into the mine the way
I'd like it to, I'd remember the other thing
as well. I'd say nothing, I can't imagine
that I would say anything
as both places changed and anyone could
support the change, it would be what I remembered
not as I wrote it, which is impossible,
neither comfortable nor even unsettled.
In thinking of where else this is true
I recall going from house to house
in reply to the sex my parents had,
sunlit rugs and marble lobbies,
birds for a second on sills—why these
things and not time with any others
a question of emphasis and of having lived.

And of the life unhad in discussions.
Waiting under that stressed tree
I'm about to speak without cleverness
about yielding, sheltering punishment
that pursues through circumstances its objects,
traces them back into custody.
I'm very much about to speak of it
though falling to the ground again,
this time away. Tomorrow then,
at the speed of an apse or robe, invited
when familiar sense fades out
and in the air behind a bent head
shafts beckon that aren't entrances.

HOW A CAT RETURNS

I am not I when my little dog sleeps
When my cat escapes I also disappear
Love is not love which makes the state strong
I love my cat and hope she returns
So few of the pronouns are amorous ones
There's a large reward for her return
She's an instrument that escaped
Through the garden and made for the hills
The map of her route is buried in time
After giving up on her I sleep
Where one sometimes recognizes
What one always knows
The cat is gone and except for the dog
I'm alone in the garden air
I know this because I'm not awake
I'm a dog in the roses of that state
It's of them that I choose to speak
Lost things that sleep grows back
My cat and my dog always sleep together
One chain lying on another
Now they can no longer make this state
So few of their chains are visible
One sometimes makes what one always loves
Love then escapes through the air
Then the air is a kind of enough
Its lines as fine as the nerves of wrens
I go on looking for miles at a time

Sometimes I put up flyers and recognize
Things done come back to speech

As things said return to behavior
So few of these things are visible
The cat lives on in photographs of her
The birds call out in the garden
Will she survive this benevolent state
I put up flyers that mention the reward
I recognize what one always knows
The dollar is alive, mild as a hill
It's a kind of enough, amorous in chains
One is a dollar or a pronoun
Lying in sleep or going on alone
The hills are visible parts of the air
They sleep together, grow mild, disappear
Are made known, restated, come back
Alone as a pronoun I too return
Wearing a dollar around my neck
Made of the chains of love and the state
The dog and cat of being amorous
I'm awake because I know this state
Where the rose escapes in things said
It's of that route I neglect to speak
While things fly nervously
One waits as the other goes away
The night for instance and the morning after

One sometimes loves what is done to one
The morning and that of the next day
Then the air is full of wrens
The cat strains at the chain, the dog behaves
The air grows dim and mild
They recognize me and I love them

IN GARDENS WHERE SAINTS MEET

there to exchange nothing other
than protean proper names, touch
a wire to the soil while
the fall quickens shifting synecdoches

where motion moves past the still
both at their most given
and these gifts of clear flames
causing no pain for an hour or two

what of them there to be said
in an autumn made examples of
everything every day a single place
undisturbed in the process of being

repeated without a progress being made
without standard text or record to protect
there where what repeats
what said in running quarantines

of two or more detained in terms
on their way out others not
yet here in a setting
slight cold returns unevenly

SENT PAST EXHIBITS

The suspending of imaginary penalties
allows a life lived to again
turn back to experience,
over a barricade into the land of Cockaigne.
Brief suspension is one of the things
the penalties often imagine.
This reprieve supposes the barricade
and the land on either side
imagines the other as Cockaigne.
Its trees move back and forth in a breeze
consisting of banisters, gates
and servants' entrances, stone steps
barely in this time and life,
boulevards lined with iron railings.
The railings cut in floral patterns
by hands now elsewhere, patterns
that are curves grown obedient
to an imagination's past.
Through these grilles other lands
imagined to be inaccessible,
the inaccessible lands
desires cross without incident
as easily as times of day.
Times themselves desires
allowed by the climb of the sun.
A sun that allows the poppy to be seen
as a throwing open of doors

and the glint of iron railings as
the arrival of an iron poppy.
An idea of iron that rises from the ground
past shadows of pedestrians
as a barricade with property behind it.
The doors of houses flaws in this
birdsong crosses through
and behind these doors the as yet unkilled
sleep in the land of Cockaigne.
Waiting there, a desire for dawn
at odds with the desire to sleep,
the pressure to become a servant builds
and the doors to both are thrown open.
Night follows night into the record,
becomes a repeating fraction, holds,
mnemonic to be heard and listened to.
The boulevards grow wider, too wide
for barricades; now the doors
of their age, always open.
Eras also have mornings and nights,
misrecognitions, strangers, goals,
gates and territorial songs of warning.
Neither these railings nor the place beyond them
is a penalty, the penalty
is being there in the imagined
asylum of evening, a barricade
without the protection of a shape.

This shapelessness Cockaigne,
an experience of experience
felt as more of the same night.
A night bright blue for a time
and the birds that traced its thoughts
were the color of iron. I noticed the chain
of myself and walked along it
using my body as a shield.
Years of this without incident.

PRIOR TO ASSENT

If I were *already* building something,
were still in the middle of it?
That would be good, I'd like that.
I remember now how dangerous
it is to be there though,
the swing through a dome, a new life
pretty hard to see in the back.
It would be good to have someone to talk to.
Then all things again
moving at once, leaving the clergy,
and inside a pen falls from the mirror.
The green time, thoughts lying down
as letters in the face of a hand.
I feel it on the tired lip,
in the repetition of a phrase—
a loyalty I more am than know
and probably why I slept so much.
Still, it would be good to have someone
to talk to, if I'm to do this thing
that goes on without me.

A CALENDAR

Often I think that certain colors move
in a room with the water rising
or are the days kept out of a speech
that only refers to horizon
and at these times it seems quite clear
it's August when I think of this
as a story less being than told
about a perverse expenditure
in which it's raining from an old life held
at the seams of the next and the rain
slows, slows and even lessens
till the center of a kind
of turning aside in modesty
at the bottom of a cup,
one extended from the soldier
to demonstrate a lake
can be offered out to someone else
who also wishes in prison to rule,
abroad to be alone in a cave,
and little by little to die
saying one thing and meaning the next.

Often I think this for hours at a time
without knowing or wanting to
yet so in search of it all the same
the slack time of a snowfall
means nothing to me, nor a short

Indian summer, alike as meeting
a stranger's brother in the street;
nor will an interview detain or move me
more than a weather report,
a person more than an animal;
when the immense thing happens it passes
through a vivid distance first
where colors were ordered to go
and I begin again the process of moving
outside and inside and through
the pain of an unknown body,
one unable to tell the difference
between its mud and another's.
Like people from a place,
having almost been there
I almost know.

WRITTEN ON A COLUMN

The different heights one wakes at where
waking is a character of the head then
given the entire morning, no sense of when
depths refreshed the windows—they're there
already, the loan lent. From out of what
old angle or plane less sure than that

the keen era in full swing and that
sense of a stifled reoccurrence where
waking would be birdsong saying what
instead is patterns of tools in a coverlet then
revealed to be limbs, the rest of the day now there
with the patience of a target. No warning when

the head became these concentric rings or when
they failed to open further—not that
such events would be easily noticed there.
Humming a work song learned where
the others are going, the morning is just then
waves of migrants moving in what

compelled style only those who know what
the language of birds is could say. And when
Sunday comes the rest remember then
forget again—this the nature of that
trough on the other side of effort somewhere,
another head. Most wake there

while those with balconies lounge there
studying to be interpreters of what
birdsong says above the market where
the others are heading. Their fate was decided when
they agreed to have one, one which looked like that
turning away of the instant now and then

still here as siesta, a sincere point that then
breaks out in the stained space there
for this purpose. A few plateaus are like that:
demeanors, sills, horizons, trials, what
the tops of heads in a crowd look like when
bobbing. Points pulled along into where

that morning's open rings recede to what
time is when it's left on a clock face, held there,
as circle then grid, from going nowhere

MIXED MODE

The experience of leaving
one category for another,
of smooth being colder
than rough and of
that December I suffer
as the experience of leaving
one category for another,
using a life that way
that opens and stops
moving, done,
furtively waving
as with one month
that opens and stops
among the others,
waiting and waking
in a place which seems filled
with restrained abilities,
that experience that
has never seemed to me
to arrive before night
except as the need
to want to live
and want to be dead,
using a life that way,
face first, name gone,
and coming to
among a rival's things

THEY MET ONLY IN THE EVENINGS

On the border the horizon adequate
to determine a sleep-spell of the other
readily and easily in all points

A discretion that should not melt
which moves the inadmissible around
persons the background

Of purposes of entrancing and acquiring
to record the terms of intimate place
under a different name to enter a veil

Upon the ground to believe the air
at any time described as outside
in proceedings within proceedings

To share the identity of greenest persons
as evening representatives
within any country spouse or convicts

To stare together with the findings
to entertain it in the mouth
of every 6 months and the name for such

A form of relief with regard to those
who would sense strains in light
the sense of all speed as may gesture

Suppleness in the system
beginning in this pose of 12 months
needed for that unfolding

Each darkness of pattern appears to be
a responsibility in the making
disclosure through relations

Affecting the compound authority
of disclosure in general
purposes at trial in solitary facts

Likely to issue in possession
if available in no voice
written later after daydreams

Of limitation flashed whole or part
grave of a power or intelligence
the intelligence foreign to power

A power falling down shall not
striking the atmosphere
the night that follows upon the first

Of purposes the powder-dusted place
it appears in writing and writing
into amber reason

The sought described in the dark
does not appear to be visitation
to slip within whoever harbors

Gray of boundaries years or both
held over in persons defined
as guests of an energy

Lived outside a flight to human life
a feeling sought for that basis
planned and carried back

Vital of harbor recognizable
suffered in the streets of events
forming calls upon calls

The basis leading days the place it appears
there are such warehouses
the future may be detained among

WALL OF MEN AND WOMEN

In that rich basin we have yet to do more
than use, open speech was declared
a needless and superfluous art; maybe later
after things were done being sent
to the wrong places, these here
and these others slipping through or gone.
It might almost have gone without saying;
the people of themselves were only after
food and water, any words that remained
less than right for the curious work
they had to do: dressing, hitting, taking.
If they'd taken the time to say something
it would have passed out among the others,
who already ridiculed it. So there was now
no more means of saying anything.
Soon the hand had every advantage
over the mouth, and as a throat's wealth
of suffering had no road out, its thoughts
were now shut up at home doing nothing.
And in this way they became excellent artists
in common, necessary things: standing aside,
looking wild, and sleeping were quite well made
by them; their face, particularly, was very much
in fashion, of a color that prevented change
from being noticed; and the shape of it was such
that the damage flowed to the sides of the screen
and only the purer part made it to the observer's eye,

which wasn't accustomed to anything else.
For this they had their lawgiver to thank,
who, in relieving the people of the trouble
of saying useless things, set them up
to show their skill in giving beauty
to objects of daily and indispensable use,
none of which were to be had, and so
for a while they were released from all kinds of action.

THE NATURE OF ENCOUNTERS

I'm already screwing up the end of the poem
with a hopeful form of forgetfulness.
Let me confess to you that I plan a perfect poem,
one written during the historical period.
Now this was a period I don't remember
and now another is coming to meet it.
This may fuck up the perfect poem I admit
I'd already planned a kind of mass for.
If I love one of the poems I love the other
no matter what period it is
but it's impossible—two of them?
The incredible speed with which these fade.
I'm reminded of other harmonious masses
and the brevity of that occupation.

Failing that, a barely restrained desire
to begin a poem whose spirit has disappeared.
They hurt each other, these poems,
every minute they celebrate their nuptials
in this period I'd forgotten about,
clearer now than before—it's autumn,
lightly at first and then pressing down
between the other two nearest seasons.
Which one is the stronger no one can say
but if it's this poem then I've fucked up.
I forgot to begin it except in the usual ways,
I didn't do anything except face the west

while it and the others passed by
exchanging whatever coordinates.

These feelings of shame caused them
to look out on the borders and beaches
where they'll be reunited with time.
It won't be too late for them
even if I don't do anything.
I've gone on a little too long already but
I wanted to tell you how boring it is
to face the sea in autumn
and address threats to the other seasons
in which the poems are refined and I'm forgotten.
I'd rather it were the other way around.
Under the trees, in the fog, the place
where the poem ceases to be is life.
Here comes the prose they warned us we'd become.

THIS PARTLY IMAGINARY TALE

You'll be asked questions, no doubt,
will bleed privacy, will be allowed to leave
only the previous moments, may
in next ones be privileged to see
the permanent dissolve, passings
of orders from one hand to another
or by a look; in any event
a chain that will concern you.
You may be let out as a means
to extend it, telling others what
you saw, worried you're affecting them,
have been sent to do just that
though it feels the opposite. It may be
that feelings haven't been accurate
instruments for some time now,
have grown compliant just at the point
where they seem unpredictable. That too
is a feeling, one that comes from having had
others, in the place they kept you
before duties became more subtly the same.
The place you still are though you may be let out
and of which you'll speak in some way
whatever you say, that they may be
distracted, thinking of their own time there,
how they left and how they got here

by similar shameful means. Together
you'll wonder how much the other knows
and how it would be if it were you,
a life like a length of rope,
or if you've been allowed to leave.

HYSTERON PROTERON

What follows are examples of all that has happened:
of that which hasn't failed to occur
in any kind of archive at all;
of that which suffers commemoration;
of a change or changes from no fixed state;
of that which occurs before I become
fatally ill, should that be what happens;
before a term not yet known fades
from use after taking hold for too long;
a flow of examples called feeling one's way,
broken sleep and friendship, the running of programs;
daylight, the invisible gardener;
sunset, an inventory of
not yet to no longer;
nights looking at the sky
of living in an empire—
strange it would extend so far,
extends so far—a product of days
if there are any of those, any part of
the bare life and sound of the group not yet
accounted for, yielded, made and trained.
In little groups of one or more
being overheard becomes lyrical politics;
goes nowhere, passes, sets;
a feeling of meeting on corners disappears
almost entirely from law and mind and
reappears precisely for that reason.

The chosen design is finished and thought of,
approved slag from which choice lifts off
like a craving in space, latest thing
about which even the poorest can have an opinion,
can only have it the way one sees
a building become a set of buildings then
leap off into the sky together;
the way one sees no longer.
Staying in love to the rhythm of bombs:
before the package hits the before fired before aimed;
it's discovered statues go on forever
when falling and when remembered just after
as right before having done so.
This is written, leaving Paris
after having come there for seven days
to celebrate the birthday of a friend;
it's described by that friend and a certain snow
blows over and under a bridge on the Seine,
heedless until explained; he begins to describe it;
Eve is claimed born across the water
and not yet proved; Eve is "made."
Now in poor taste to have thoughts,
think of having them, do anything other
than receive announcements meant for anyone,
perfect a current in the set of the mouth,
feel of being ruled from inside and out,
the stung thought of skin from either side.

The new plans are unveiled;
a year of gavels coming down;
all the unrelated deaths
which can't seem to help coming after;
falling in love to the news of bombs,
multiply helpless, ebbing to a future.
The related deaths are related;
some last calls to loved ones are overheard,
some of them overt, some relying
on knowledge to come, all overt
in adding last moments
to a mutual past, soon everyone's.
The metaphors fall from the sky,
survived by a concerned, professional tone;
narrations as far from revulsion as pleasure;
the buildings fall, the other then the one,
like a craving in space, a new language:
the fortuitous encounter on a sky
of two planes and two towers;
some last calls to loved ones are made;
an inaudible change in destination;
a morning advancing east to west,
revealing the east or taking back the west.
911 Is a Joke, How Can I Move
the Crowd, Police and Thieves, The Ocean.
What is the meaning of a
pure series of interruptions?

A screaming comes across the sky;
the metaphors go up and the towers are built;
Paul Celan enters the life of the Seine;
saying butterfly crying being
born in Beth Israel; being made.
Todesfuge; after the first
death there is no other; I am going
to write it for you; cracks and reforms and bursts
in the violet air; the figure 5
in gold on a red fire truck
moving tense unheeded; Sunday
Morning's first stanza; decorative
arts: The Dream of John Ball;
the fortuitous encounter on a dissecting table
of a sewing machine and an umbrella.
The sea whisper'd; I prefer not to;
Ozymandias and Darien;
Fourier reads Sade and begins
to believe that pleasure is a butterfly,
self-interest a flower in the garden;
they take their solitary way.
Flowers freaked with jet; Landscape with Fall
of Icarus and Children's Games;
John Ball dies; John Ball writes
a letter to the countryside
and is born; Dante's arrow hits
the target; the black stone is worshipped,

shattered, worshipped, polished, found.
"Before all that can be called 'before' "
is written, copied, written, copied, found;
and that advice on the battlefield of spring,
in Mantua, when the bees return to the saffron flowers.
I hate and I love . . . I feel it happening and;
letters, suddenly allowed
separate realms of sound;
the unfinished tower,
like a craving in language, is thought to exist,
abandoned, worked on, begins to be built;
"Eve" is born; "Eve" is claimed and made.
All fall narratives including the sun;
pronouns, now, this place then;
clouds in the water, love of the future

TO CLASSES

I am that member of the family of things
that never leaves the house again
and steps into war church each hour
That corresponds to images and on
the street your face and body and clothes
your walk and silky destinations
Without knowing it I digest your choices
and forget to connect you to the rest
You in whom the years have changed
You both a block and its veins, the portion
path to the places that are gone to
The music is going if there is music
There's always some sound or other
Signs of effort on the face of the air
There are those who wait in longing to hear
and those around whom dead waves flow
It's like twilight to be alive now

TEXT
9.5/15 Scala

DISPLAY
Bank Gothic

DESIGNER
J.G. Braun

COMPOSITOR
BookMatters, Berkeley

PRINTER + BINDER
Friesens Corporation